Documenting EARLY AMERICA

Understanding the
Declaration of Independence

Sally Senzell Isaacs

Crabtree Publishing Company
www.crabtreebooks.com

Author: Sally Senzell Isaacs
Editor-in-Chief: Lionel Bender
Editor: Kelley MacAulay
Proofreaders: Adrianna Morganelli,
    Crystal Sikkens
Project editor: Robert Walker
Photo research: Susannah Jayes
Designer: Malcolm Smythe
Production coordinator: Katherine Kantor
Production: Kim Richardson
Prepress technician: Margaret Amy Salter
Consultant: Professor Richard Jensen,
    history teacher, consultant, and author

This book was produced for
    Crabtree Publishing Company
    by Bender Richardson White, U.K.

Cover:
Thomas Jefferson Memorial in Washington, D.C.,

Title page:
Presenting the Declaration of Independence to Congress

Photographs:
© Art Archive: Chateau de Berancourt/Gianni Dagli Orti: p. 20
© Corbis: Bettmann: p. 21, 27, 28
© iStockphoto.com: p. 16, 23 (left and right), 29
© Library of Congress: p. 22 (ppmsa 08314)
© Northwind Picture Archives: p. 1, 4, 5, 6, 7, 8, 9, 11, 12, 13, 14, 15, 17, 18, 19, 24, 25, 26
© Shutterstock.com: cover
© The Granger Collection: p. 10

Library and Archives Canada Cataloguing in Publication

Isaacs, Sally Senzell, 1950-
    Understanding the Declaration of Independence / Sally Senzell Isaacs.

(Documenting early America)
Includes index.
ISBN 978-0-7787-4371-2 (bound).--ISBN 978-0-7787-4376-7 (pbk.)

    1. United States. Declaration of Independence--Juvenile literature.
2. United States--Politics and government--1775-1783--Juvenile literature.
3. United States--History--Colonial period, ca. 1600-1775--Juvenile
literature. 4. United States--History--Revolution, 1775-1783--Juvenile
literature. I. Title. II. Series: Isaacs, Sally Senzell, 1950- . Documenting
early America.

E221.I83 2008   j973.3'13   C2008-905557-8

Library of Congress Cataloging-in-Publication Data

Isaacs, Sally Senzell, 1950-
    Understanding the Declaration of Independence / Sally Senzell Isaacs.
        p. cm. -- (Documenting early America)
    Includes index.
    ISBN-13: 978-0-7787-4376-7 (pbk. : alk. paper)
    ISBN-10: 0-7787-4376-4 (pbk. : alk. paper)
    ISBN-13: 978-0-7787-4371-2 (reinforced library binding : alk. paper)
    ISBN-10: 0-7787-4371-3 (reinforced library binding : alk. paper)
    1. United States. Declaration of Independence--Juvenile literature. 2.
United States--Politics and government--1775-1783--Juvenile literature. 3.
United States--History--Colonial period, ca. 1600-1775--Juvenile
literature. 4. United States--History--Revolution, 1775-1783--Juvenile
literature. I. Title. II. Series.

    E221.I83 2009
    973.3--dc22
                                2008036595

Crabtree Publishing Company

www.crabtreebooks.com   1-800-387-7650

Published in Canada
Crabtree Publishing
616 Welland Ave.
St. Catharines, Ontario
L2M 5V6

Published in the United States
Crabtree Publishing
PMB16A
350 Fifth Ave., Suite 3308
New York, NY 10118

Published in the United Kingdom
Crabtree Publishing
White Cross Mills
High Town, Lancaster
LA1 4XS

Published in Australia
Crabtree Publishing
386 Mt. Alexander Rd.
Ascot Vale (Melbourne)
VIC 3032

Contents

A Very Big Step

The Declaration of Independence is one of the most important writings in the history of the United States. It was written and signed more than 230 years ago in 1776. Before that time, there was no country called the United States of America. There were 13 American **colonies** that belonged to Britain. The people in the colonies were British **subjects**. They followed laws made in Britain.

◄ *The Declaration of Independence was written on parchment paper, made from animal skin.*

Making a very big decision

In 1776, the American colonies declared their
independence. That means they told King George III of
Britain that they did not want to be part of his country.
They wanted to start a country of their own. The men
who signed the **Declaration** took a big risk. Would the
king punish them? Would they be able to build a new
country on their own?

▼ *This map shows the United States as it*
was before the Declaration of Independence.

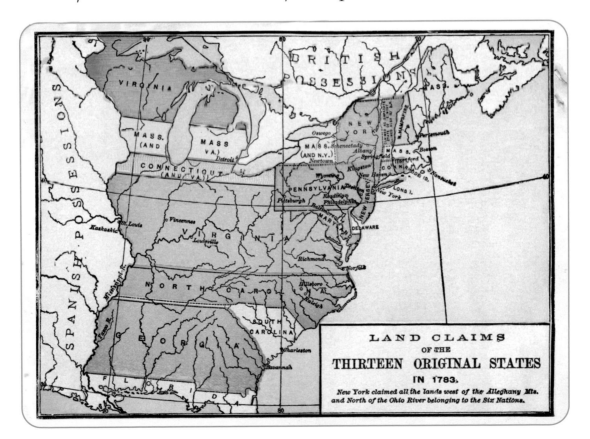

LAND CLAIMS
OF THE
THIRTEEN ORIGINAL STATES
IN 1783.
New York claimed all the lands west of the Alleghany Mts.
and North of the Ohio River belonging to the Six Nations.

Life in the Colonies

Around 1600, some Europeans moved to America and created the colonies. Many of them moved to the colonies for a better life. They wanted freedom that they did not have in Europe. They wanted a chance to own land and practice their own religions. In the colonies, most people lived on small farms. They had pigs and cows. They grew their own food, and chose their own leaders. People who lived in the colonies were called **colonists**.

Slaves
Many people did not choose to come to the colonies—they were forced to come. These people were **slaves**. A slave is owned by another person and is usually made to work for little or no pay.

▼ *Colonists built schools for their children.*

Ruled by Britain

The country of Britain was in charge of the 13 colonies. Even though Britain was very far away from the colonies, the colonists had to follow Britain's laws. They also had to pay **taxes** to Britain. A tax is money that people pay the government to run their country. King George III sent soldiers and officials to the colonies. They made sure the colonists obeyed the laws and paid the taxes.

◄ *George III was Britain's king from 1760 to 1820.*

The Terrible Taxes

By 1765, many colonists grew unhappy with Britain. The trouble was taxes! Britain needed money. It recently fought a war with France that had cost a lot of money. Britain's lawmakers, called the **Parliament**, wanted the colonists to pay for part of that war. Therefore, Parliament voted to make the colonists pay more taxes.

◄ *In local stores, colonists had to pay more money for their cloth, newspapers, sugar, and tea because of Britain's taxes.*

No representation

Colonists had to pay extra tax every time they bought everyday items such as tea and cloth. This made them angry. The colonists felt that they should decide what taxes they pay, not people in Britain. The lawmakers in Parliament were **representatives** of the British people. People choose representatives to speak for them when laws are made. The colonists did not have representatives in Parliament. There was no one in Parliament who would defend their rights.

▼ *These colonists formed a group called the Sons of Liberty. They were angry about* "taxation without representation."

The Colonies Act

The colonists were angry about *"taxation without representation."* Many of them stopped buying British tea. They made their own cloth instead of buying cloth from British stores. They wrote letters to the king. The letters said the taxes were unfair. King George III continued to tax the colonists, however.

The Boston Tea Party
One night in 1773, some colonists, dressed as Native Americans, climbed onto a British ship in the Boston Harbor. They threw boxes of tea into the water and ruined the tea so nobody could drink it. The incident became known as the Boston Tea Party. The king was angry! He closed the Boston Harbor so that no ships could deliver goods until the colonists paid for the lost tea.

▲ *Women stopped buying British cloth. They spun wool into yarn and made their own cloth.*

▼ *This is Carpenter's Hall, Philadelphia, where the First Congress was held.*

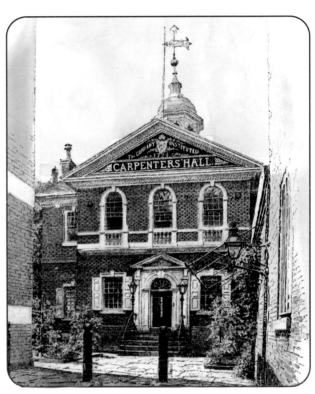

Looking for a better way

On September 5, 1774, each colony sent representatives to a meeting in Carpenter's Hall in Philadelphia. The meeting was called the First Continental **Congress**. It was a type of Parliament. The representatives were all men. They hoped to find a way to get along with Britain. They met several times. They sent more letters to King George III. They also asked colonists to stop buying British goods.

War Begins!

A battle with Britain broke out in Massachusetts in April 1775. After that, there was little hope to work things out with King George III. On April 19, British soldiers headed to the villages of Lexington and Concord. They heard that colonial soldiers were collecting guns and gunpowder. The colonial soldiers called themselves **minutemen** because they could be ready to fight in a minute. No one knows who fired first, but soon a battle was raging.

An American leader
A Second Continental Congress met in May of 1775. John Adams, from Massachusetts, wanted to form an American army. Others agreed. They chose a man who spoke like a leader to be the general in charge of the new army. His name was George Washington.

▲ *After George Washington led the Continental Army, he became the first **president** of the United States.*

The British are coming

When the British soldiers arrived in Lexington, the minutemen met them with their guns. Before long, eight minutemen were dead. This was the first battle of a very bloody war between the colonists and Britain. The war lasted for six years. It is called the Revolutionary War or the American **Revolution**. A revolution is a strong move by people to change their **government**. A government is a group of leaders who run a country.

▼ *In the battle at Lexington, about 70 minutemen fought against almost 700 British soldiers.*

Talk of Independence

Every day, more colonists turned against the king. They wanted to break away from Britain and start their own country. Colonists who fought for independence from Britain were called **Patriots**.

In 1776, Thomas Paine wrote a book called *Common Sense*. It gave common-sense reasons why independence was the best thing for the American colonies. After reading the book, many people from the colonies agreed with the Patriots that they should fight for independence.

In secret
On November 9, 1775, the men in Congress signed a Resolution of Secrecy. They promised to keep their plans a secret. It said that anyone who broke the promise must leave Congress as *"an enemy to the liberties of America."*

▲ *Patriot Patrick Henry made a speech exclaiming, "Give me liberty or give me death!"*

The Famous Five

By June 1776, the Continental Congress stopped writing pleading letters to the king. They started talking about independence. Richard Henry Lee asked the Congress to vote on a statement saying *"these United Colonies are … free and independent States."* Congress voted yes.

A group of five men started planning a Declaration of Independence. The group was called the Committee of Five.

▼ *The Committee of Five were (left to right)*
Benjamin Franklin, Thomas Jefferson, Roger Sherman,
John Adams, and Robert R. Livingston.

Jefferson's Job

The Committee of Five asked Thomas Jefferson to take over writing the Declaration. Jefferson was a lawyer from Virginia. He was interested in everything from science to music. He was especially interested in creating a government that protects the rights of its people.

▲ *Thomas Jefferson drew all the plans for his house in Virginia. The house is called Monticello. You can visit the house today.*

Putting it in writing

Jefferson wrote the Declaration of Independence by himself. It took him 17 days. He wanted colonists to hear the words and agree that it was time for independence from Britain. He wanted the king—and the rest of the world—to realize why the colonies were breaking away.

Jefferson's reasons for independence

- The king has been unfair to the colonists.
- People have rights that cannot be taken away by kings.
- A government should protect the people's rights.
- A government should listen to its people.

▶ *Jefferson (standing) discussed his ideas with Franklin and Adams before writing them down with quill and ink.*

God-given Rights

The most famous words of the Declaration are *"We hold these truths to be self-evident that all men are created equal."*

A self-evident truth is one that is always true. It is a truth that cannot be changed by any person. For example, another self-evident truth is, *"The ocean is wet."* The Declaration of Independence declares that all people are equal. A king is no better than a poor shoemaker.

▲ *The Declaration said that these businessmen were no better than farmers and no worse than colonial leaders.*

A long wait for equality
Today people question Jefferson's ideas of equality. At the time of the Declaration, women, Native Americans, and African Americans did not have the same rights as white men, and Jefferson was not worried by this. For example, they could not vote for colonial leaders. They didn't get those rights for many more years.

Freedom for all

Jefferson wrote that God gave rights to everyone. These are rights to life and **liberty** and the right to find happiness. Liberty is another word for "freedom."

The Declaration says that a government should make sure that people have these rights. Jefferson believed that people should create the government. People should choose their leaders and their laws.

Failed by Britain

In the Declaration, Jefferson wanted to explain how King George III was hurting the colonists. King George III had stopped the colonies from trading with other countries, and prevented colonists from making decisions on many things in their towns. He had sent soldiers to punish the colonists who spoke against him. The soldiers burned down homes and other buildings.

▼ *British soldiers arrived by ship in New York.*

Trying times

The king also forced the colonists to let the British soldiers live in their houses. He even paid soldiers from Germany to go to the colonies to fight the Patriots. At the same time, there were the king's high taxes! The Declaration says that the king *"destroyed the lives of our people."*

Then Jefferson explained that the colonists had really tried to work things out. They had sent many letters. They had asked the British people for help. However, the British people and the king were *"deaf to the voice of justice."*

◄ *In Boston, some Patriots were so angry that they caught British tax collectors and covered them in tar and feathers to protest against King George III and his laws.*

Free States

What happens when a government is very unfair to its people? What if it will not change its ways? Jefferson believed that in these situations people have the right to bring about change. In the Declaration, he wrote that people have a right to start a new government that can give them *"safety and happiness."* This is what the Patriots were fighting for.

▶ *This is the Declaration of Independence that was drafted by Jefferson. There are many areas where he crossed out text while trying to write a version that everyone would accept.*

22

Claiming independence

In the last part of the Declaration of Independence, Jefferson declared that the colonies were no longer part of Britain. He wrote that *"these United Colonies are ... free and independent states."* They had the power to do everything that independent **states** had a right to do, such as creating their own laws and government. Finally, at the end of the Declaration, the colonies pledged to **unite**, or join together, and help one another. Here, Jefferson used the words *"United States of America"* for the first time.

▶ *Starting in 1775, Congress met in this building in Philadelphia, later called Independence Hall.*

▼ *One of the first United States flags had 13 stars and 13 stripes to represent the 13 colonies.*

An Important Vote

On June 28, 1776, Jefferson finished writing the Declaration. On July 4, Congress met to vote on whether it would accept the document. The Declaration was read. Representatives of South Carolina and Georgia asked to have one part of the Declaration crossed out before they would accept it. The part they wanted crossed out said that the king was wrong to allow slavery. Many people in South Carolina and Georgia owned slaves, so they would not agree to this.

◄ *New Yorkers who wanted independence pulled down a statue of King George III.*

▲ *John Trumball painted this picture of the Committee of Five as they presented the Declaration to Congress.*

The U.S.A. is born

When the Declaration was finished, representatives stood up one by one and voted "yes" to independence. When they voted "yes," a new country was born called the United States of America. The people were called Americans. That day, John Hancock, the president of the Congress, and Charles Thomson, Congress secretary, signed the Declaration. Later, the rest of the 56 men signed it, too. They were all very brave. If America lost the Revolution, the king would likely punish them.

Spread the Word!

America was independent! It was time to share the news with the colonists. After the vote on July 4, the Declaration was given to John Dunlap. He was a printer in Philadelphia. Dunlap worked through the night. He made copies of the Declaration on his printing presses. Messengers brought copies to soldiers fighting the war. They brought other copies to the villages and towns. On July 8, the Declaration was read to the public for the first time. Americans celebrated when they heard the news.

▼ *People gathered to hear the Declaration of Independence.*

The Declaration today

Twenty-five of those first copies of the Declaration of Independence still exist today. The signed document is sealed under glass in Washington, D.C. It sits in a building called the National Archives. The air and temperature under the glass are set to preserve the special paper. Millions of visitors come to see the Declaration every year. It is a symbol of liberty.

▼ *People are welcome to view the Declaration of Independence in the National Archives building in Washington, D.C.*

The Words Live On

The words of the Declaration of Independence are even more important than the well-guarded piece of paper on which they are written. The words have been remembered through history. In 1858, Abraham Lincoln spoke out against slavery. He said that the Declaration promised life, liberty, and happiness to all men equally. These rights belonged to slaves, too. When Lincoln became president of the United States, he ended slavery.

◄ *In 1963, Dr. Martin Luther King, Jr. spoke to a crowd of about 250,000 people in Washington, D.C. He talked about the need for equality for African Americans.*

Equality for all

In 1848, Elizabeth Cady Stanton and others held a
meeting for women's rights in Seneca Falls, New York. The
women wrote a declaration for women's rights. The first
part of it sounded like the Declaration of Independence.
They said, *"all men and women are created equal,"* though.

Today, Americans are free people. They choose their
leaders and lawmakers. They are free to speak out against
their government. The people can always work to make
changes for the better.

▼ *Across America, people celebrate Independence Day every July 4.*

Timeline

1600 People from Europe start coming to America

1765 Britain's Parliament passes the Stamp Act, making colonists pay taxes on newspapers and legal papers

1773 Angry about a tea tax, Boston Patriots dump tea in the harbor (Boston Tea Party)

1774 The First Continental Congress meets in Philadelphia

1775 First shots of the American Revolution are fired in April, in Lexington and Concord, Massachusetts

1775 The Second Continental Congress chooses George Washington to lead their army

1776 On July 4, the Continental Congress agrees to the Declaration of Independence. The United States of America is born

1776 On July 8, the Declaration of Independence is first read in public

1781 The British armies are defeated and fighting ends

1783 A peace treaty ends the American Revolution

Websites

1. Ben's Guide to U.S. Government for Kids
http://bensguide.gpo.gov/3-5/documents/declaration/index.html
This site includes the complete text of the Declaration and links to related subject areas.

2. UShistory.org
http://www.ushistory.org/Declaration/
On this site, you will find a timeline and profiles of all 56 signers of the Declaration, as well as links to sites about events and issues related to the Declaration.

3. History.com
http://www.history.com/minisite.do?content_type=mini_home&mini_id=1056
This site includes clear explanations of each section of the Declaration, and a quiz to help you remember what you've learned.

4. The Declaration Home Page
http://www.duke.edu/eng169s2/group1/lex3/firstpge.htm
Visit this site to see early drafts of the Declaration, passages that were removed from the final version, and a "hypertext" Declaration—click on highlighted phrases and passages to find out how they developed.

5. National Archives and Records Administration
http://www.archives.gov/exhibits/charters/declaration.html
Here you will find a transcript of the Declaration, an image of the original document, and links to other websites of interest.

Further Reading

Burgan, Michael. *The Declaration of Independence*. Mankato, Minn.: Compass Point, 2001.

Gillis, Jennifer Blizin. Life in Colonial Boston. Chicago: Heinemann, 2003.

Isaacs, Sally Senzell. *America in the Time of George Washington*. Chicago: Heinemann-Raintree Library, 1999.

Marcovitz, Hal. *The Declaration of Independence*. Philadelphia: Mason Crest, 2002.

Penner, Lucille Recht. *Liberty! How the Revolutionary War Began*. New York: Random House, 2002.

Rosen, Daniel. *Independence Now: The American Revolution 1763–1783*. Washington, D.C.: National Geographic, 2004.

Swain, Gwenyth. *Declaring Freedom: A Look at the Declaration of Independence, the Bill of Rights, and the Constitution*. Minneapolis: Lerner, 2004.

Glossary

colonist Someone who lives in a colony

colony A place where people live that is far from the country that rules it

congress A meeting of representatives to discuss a subject; the lawmakers

declaration Something that is told or read to many people

government The people who run a country or colony

independence Able to govern oneself

liberty Freedom

minutemen Colonial soldiers who said they could get ready to fight the British in a minute

Parliament The lawmaking group for Britain

Patriot A person in America who fought for independence from Britain

president The elected leader of the government or an organization

representative Someone who speaks for many people when laws are made

revolution A strong move by people to change their government

slave A person who is owned by another person and must work for that person without pay

state A part of a nation, with its own laws and government

subjects People who are controlled by a leader or a state

tax Money that people pay to run their government

unite Join together

Index

Printed in the U.S.A. – BG